W9-AJS-487

NATURE'S MYSTERIES

HOW CATERPILLARS TURN INTO BUTTERFLIES

Jill Bailey

BENCHMARK BOOKS

MARSHALL CAVENDISH
NEW YORK

Benchmark Books
Marshall Cavendish Corporation
99 White Plains Road
Tarrytown, New York 10591-9001

Series created by Discovery Books

Library of Congress Cataloging-in-Publication Data
Bailey, Jill
    How caterpillars turn into butterflies/Jill Bailey
    p.   cm. - (Nature's mysteries)
    Includes bibliographical references (p.) and index
    Summary: Describes the life cycle of the butterfly, from the hatching of the caterpillar, through its struggle to survive, to its metamorphosis into a butterfly and the laying of its own eggs.
    ISBN 0-7614-0857-6
    1. Butterflies - Metamorphosis - Juvenile literature. 2. Caterpillars - Juvenile literature. [1. Caterpillars. 2. Butterflies. 3. Metamorphosis] I. Title. II. Series.
    QL544.2.B36 1998   98-10528 CIP AC
    595.78'139-DC21

Printed in Hong Kong

Acknowledgments
Text consultant: Susan Borkin, Milwaukee Public Museum
Illustrated by Stuart Lafford
The publishers would like to thank the following for their permission to reproduce photographs: cover John Shaw/Bruce Coleman, title page D.G. Fox/Oxford Scientific Films, 4 E. & D. Hosking/FLPA, 5 Kim Taylor/Bruce Coleman, 7 top Jens Rydell/Bruce Coleman, 22 bottom Herbert Cyron/Okapia/Oxford Scientific Films, 8 Kevin Rushby/Bruce Coleman, 9 J.A.L. Cooke/Oxford Scientific Films, 11 top P. & W. Ward/Oxford Scientific Films, 11 bottom D.G. Fox/Oxford Scientific Films, 12 Michael Fogden/Oxford Scientific Films, 13 top Kim Taylor/Bruce Coleman, 13 bottom K.G. Preston-Mafham/Premaphotos Wildlife, 14 bottom Kim Taylor/Bruce Coleman, 14 top Mantis Wildlife Films/Oxford Scientific Films, 15 John Shaw/Bruce Coleman, 16 bottom Ray Coleman/Photo Researchers/Oxford Scientific Films, 16 top J.H. Robinson/Photo Researchers/Oxford Scientific Films, 17 G.I. Bernard/Oxford Scientific Films, 18 Jane Burton/Bruce Coleman, 19 Kjell B. Sandved/Oxford Scientific Films, 20 Jane Burton/Bruce Coleman, 21 top Kim Taylor/Bruce Coleman, 21 bottom Jane Burton/Bruce Coleman, 22 J.S & E.J. Woolmer/Oxford Scientific Films, 23 top D. Maslowski/FLPA, 23 bottom Gunter Ziesler/Bruce Coleman, 24 Owen Newman/Oxford Scientific Films, 25 top Dr. Frieder Sauer/Bruce Coleman, 25 bottom K.G. Preston-Mafham/Premaphotos Wildlife, 26 Michael Fogden/Oxford Scientific Films, 27 top K.G. Preston-Mafham/Premaphotos Wildlife, 27 bottom Kjell B. Sandved/Photo Researchers/Oxford Scientific Films, 28 Dr. Eckart Pott/Bruce Coleman, 29 Stephen Dalton/Oxford Scientific Films.

(Cover) A monarch butterfly on a daisy.

CONTENTS

BUTTERFLIES AND MOTHS

There are over 150,000 different kinds of butterflies and moths in the world. They range from giants like the Hercules moth of tropical Australia, with a wingspan of up to 14.5 inches (360 millimeters), and the Queen Alexandra's bird wing butterfly of Papua New Guinea, with a wingspan of over 11 inches (280 mm), to a tiny moth from the Canary Islands with a wingspan of only 0.08 inches (2 mm).

▲ *Bird wing butterflies are common in Southeast Asia. The common bird wing may have a wingspan of 5 inches (12.5 centimeters). Many of its rarer relatives are collectors' items.*

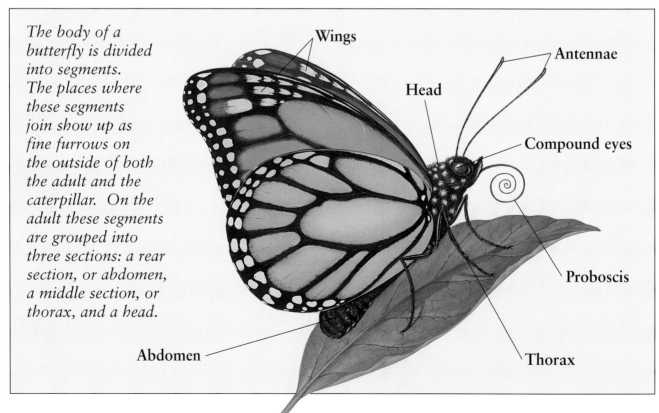

The body of a butterfly is divided into segments. The places where these segments join show up as fine furrows on the outside of both the adult and the caterpillar. On the adult these segments are grouped into three sections: a rear section, or abdomen, a middle section, or thorax, and a head.

Wings

Head

Antennae

Compound eyes

Proboscis

Abdomen

Thorax

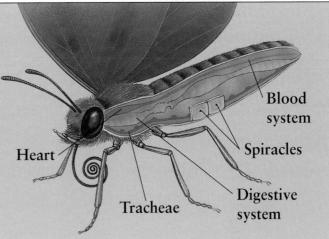

Butterflies do not have a system of arteries and veins like those of humans. An open-ended tubular "heart" pumps blood from one end of the butterfly to the other, however, setting up a flow of blood around the whole body to bathe the organs and tissues. Air circulates around the body through a network of tiny tubes (tracheae) that open to the outside through tiny holes, called spiracles, in the sides of the body. There is not much of a digestive system, as most butterflies eat very little.

Heart

Tracheae

Blood system

Spiracles

Digestive system

Moths are far more numerous than butterflies, but we see less of them because they come out mainly at night. It is the butterflies that attract our attention, with wings that display every color of the rainbow as well as colors that are visible to other animals but not to humans. Some tropical butterflies are almost as big as dinner plates, with shimmering colors that flash as they fly. Many have long been collectors' items, and some have even been made into jewelry.

Some butterflies and moths are found in the Arctic. Many migrate thousands of miles with the changing seasons. A few can fly at over fifty miles per hour (eighty kilometers per hour). Moths can find their way in near darkness, and their aerobatic maneuvers can even outwit the bats that chase them.

▼ Most moths come out only at night. This elephant hawk moth is night feeding on honeysuckle.

METAMORPHOSIS

If asked to describe a baby butterfly, you might have a difficult time coming up with an answer. The young of butterflies and moths are quite unlike their parents. They are grub-like caterpillars, with soft bodies and short, stumpy legs. Caterpillars spend their whole lives just eating and growing, until eventually they secrete a hard shell around themselves and emerge some time later as fully formed adult insects—butterflies. This great change is called metamorphosis (Greek for "change in form"). A similar transformation occurs in some other insects, such as beetles, flies, and mosquitoes. A more gradual change, which is seen in the young of grasshoppers, is called incomplete or partial metamorphosis.

Not all insects metamorphose. The silverfish that scuttle in damp corners of the kitchen are similar to the first insects that ever evolved. The young hatch from the eggs looking like miniature adults and simply grow bigger, with no metamorphosis taking place at all.

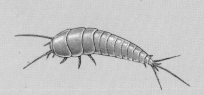
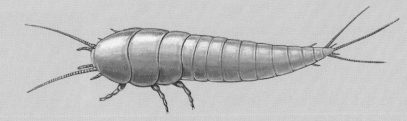

A young grasshopper nymph looks similar to its parents, but it has no wings. Gradually, wing buds form on the thorax and slowly grow into full-sized wings. This change is called partial or incomplete metamorphosis.

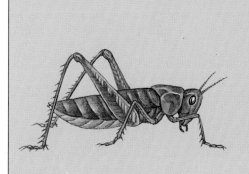
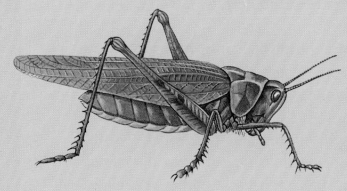

wings or good eyesight. It can put all its energy into growing, so it can grow very fast. Its soft form can expand with the development of the complex butterfly. The metamorphosis from caterpillar to butterfly serves this animal very well indeed.

A swallowtail butterfly caterpillar, left, and its adult form, below. A young animal like the caterpillar, which is very different from its parents, is called a larva. The change from caterpillar to butterfly is called complete metamorphosis. Metamorphosis is not just a change in shape; it permits caterpillars and adults to have different lifestyles. Caterpillars have hard mouth parts for feeding on tough plant leaves, while butterflies have a sucking proboscis and feed only on liquid food, such as nectar. Caterpillars cannot travel far, but butterflies can roam vast distances.

This life cycle is very complicated, but it has great advantages for both the caterpillar and the adult. For example, because caterpillars and butterflies feed on different kinds of plants, the young and the adults do not have to compete for food. Also, the butterfly needs to fly some distance to find a mate and to find new food plants on which to lay her eggs. Because butterflies can fly, they can colonize new areas. The complex structures of the butterfly's body—its wings, jointed legs, compound eyes, and antennae—take a lot of energy to produce. The simple caterpillar does not need to move far from its food plant, so it doesn't need strong legs and

FROM EGG TO CATERPILLAR

A butterfly's egg may seem very small, but in relation to the insect's size it is actually very large—thousands of times larger than a newly fertilized human egg. The eggs of butterflies and moths are usually dull in color, often laid on the undersides of leaves, among the scales of buds or in the crevices of bark, out of sight of predators. A few, like the eggs of the cabbage white butterfly, are brightly colored, usually yellow or orange. These contain bad-tasting or poisonous substances, and the bright colors advertise this fact. Some eggs may rest for the whole winter before developing, but this is rare. Usually an egg starts to develop as soon as it is laid.

A Malay lacewing butterfly lays her eggs. A special organ at the tip of the abdomen, the ovipositor, controls the position of each egg, aided by touch and taste sensors. Many butterflies and moths lay large numbers of eggs to ensure that some survive. Others lay far fewer, larger eggs with more yolk, which, if they hatch, will develop into larger larvae that are better able to survive.

Like all living things, caterpillars are made up of tiny parts called cells. What is interesting about the caterpillar story, however, is that some cells that will eventually develop into parts of the adult butterfly are already present inside the growing larvae just a few hours after the eggs are laid. They play no part in the life

A cabbage white larva bites its way out of the egg to crawl off in search of food. Many caterpillars eat the remains of their egg case before moving off. Some species will die if deprived of their egg case.

of the caterpillar, but they are preprogrammed, just waiting to take their part in the dramatic change that is to come.

THE CATERPILLAR'S WORLD

The caterpillar's world is a very small one: it is concerned with little beyond the leaf on which it is feeding. Its simple eyes are called stemmata. Each has a tiny lens that, together with the other stemmata, provides only a coarse mosaic picture, probably in black-and-white. The stemmata are important in detecting changes in light intensity, so they give the caterpillar clues about the time and length of the day. The hairs on its body are sensitive to touch and also to sound waves and vibrations. Taste and smell sensors are scattered over its cuticle. They help it find food and tell the difference between edible and poisonous leaves.

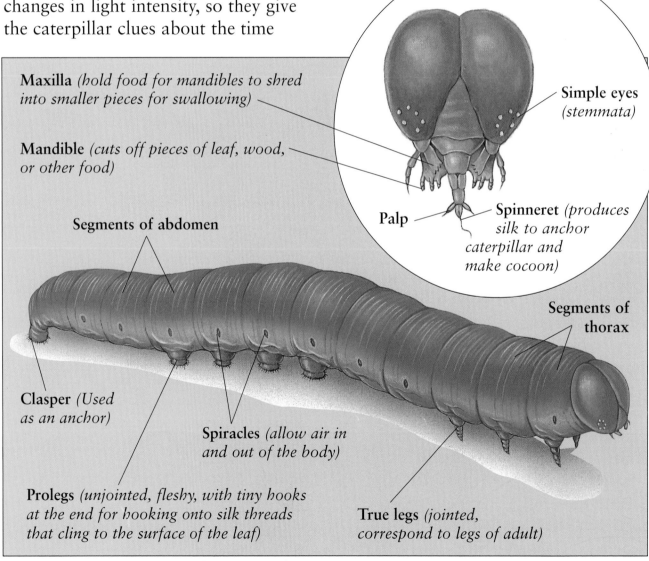

Head

Simple eyes (*stemmata*)

Palp

Spinneret (*produces silk to anchor caterpillar and make cocoon*)

Maxilla (*hold food for mandibles to shred into smaller pieces for swallowing*)

Mandible (*cuts off pieces of leaf, wood, or other food*)

Segments of abdomen

Segments of thorax

Clasper (*Used as an anchor*)

Spiracles (*allow air in and out of the body*)

Prolegs (*unjointed, fleshy, with tiny hooks at the end for hooking onto silk threads that cling to the surface of the leaf*)

True legs (*jointed, correspond to legs of adult*)

▲ A caterpillar's body is like a balloon filled with water: its shape is determined by the pressure of the fluids inside it. Its muscles push against these fluids, just as your hand can squeeze the balloon. Its stumpy little prolegs have sucker-like pads with tiny hooks for gripping silk.

Most caterpillars feed on leaves, flowers, or buds— some on only one kind of plant, others on many. A few, such as the leopard moth larva, can eat wood and spend their lives in the tunnels they make through wood or bark. There are also some strange specialists. One moth larva eats only antlers; another, which burrows into beans, is what makes Mexican jumping beans jump. The European large blue butterfly larva lives in ants' nests, feeding on the ants' larvae.

Eating is the caterpillar's main purpose. Caterpillars are among the greediest feeders in the world. The North American polyphemus moth caterpillar eats 86,000 times its own birth-weight during its first fifty-six days of life. This is equivalent to a human baby consuming over 280 tons of food. A fully grown carpenterworm moth larva is 72,000 times bigger than a newly hatched one.

▼ A looper caterpillar, or inchworm, looks as if it is measuring the ground one inch (2.54 centimeters) at a time. To move forward, it stretches out its body and puts down its true legs. Then it hangs on with these while it draws up the prolegs at the back to meet them.

ENEMIES OF CATERPILLARS

Caterpillars have many enemies. Among them are birds, who find caterpillars the perfect soft food for their young, and small insect-eating mammals and lizards. Many insects, such as praying mantises, beetles, and even ants, prey on caterpillars. Parasitic wasps lay their eggs in caterpillars, and their larvae eat away at them from the inside.

Caterpillars have evolved a huge range of defenses, some of them quite unexpected. The simplest is to feed on the underside of the leaf or at night, out of sight of predators. Some bind a leaf around themselves with the silk they spin. Others feed in large groups under a silken tent. Even if an enemy sees through the tent, it is unlikely to take all the caterpillars. Bagworm moth larvae spin a case around themselves and build in pieces of dead leaf and twigs for disguise. Other larvae simply escape by dropping to the ground on a silken thread.

This caterpillar is mimicking a snake. When alarmed, it puffs up the segments just below its head to show off two large eye-like spots, which look as if they belong to a much larger animal.

Stinging hairs and spiny bodies are another common defense. Many caterpillars have camouflage colors or even resemble a lifeless (and therefore inedible) object, such as a twig or dead leaf.

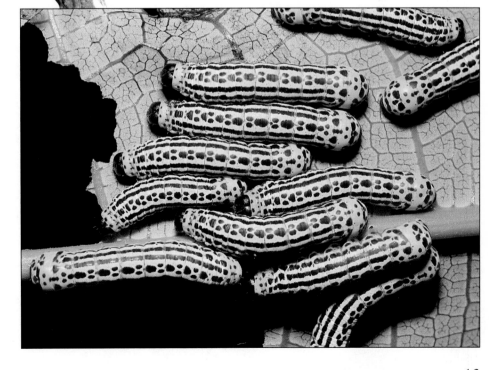

◄ The caterpillar of the oak beauty moth resembles an oak twig. It usually remains quite still by day, relying on camouflage for protection, and does not move off to feed until darkness falls.

Caterpillars also have to cope with hostile plants that produce poisonous or bad-tasting chemicals in their leaves. Some caterpillars, such as those of the monarch butterfly and smoky moths, can cope with these and store them in their bodies for their own defense. Such caterpillars often have bright warning colors and patterns, usually black and red, orange, or yellow.

Some are disguised as bird droppings. Others mimic snakes, puffing up their backs to reveal huge eye-like markings and even hissing at their attackers.

▶ These caterpillars appear to have heads at both ends of their bodies. Attacking birds are quite likely to peck at the caterpillar's rear, where they do less damage.

CHANGING SIZE AND SHAPE

Like their parents, caterpillars are covered by a cuticle. This makes it difficult to expand as they grow. From time to time they shed their "skins" in a process called molting. First the brain releases a special chemical messenger, a molting hormone. A new, soft cuticle forms below the old one. The old one is partially broken down, and its nutrients are used to make the new cuticle.

▶ *This monarch butterfly larva is about to turn into a pupa. It has anchored itself to a stem by a little silk pad, to which it hooks the claws of its last segment. The old skin splits at a line of weakness over the thorax. Now it will rest until the adult butterfly is ready to emerge.*

Then the caterpillar stops feeding and may hang head-down, anchoring itself to a silk pad that it has spun. Muscles in its abdomen pump the body fluid into the thorax, building up a pressure that splits the old cuticle along a line where it is extremely thin.

◀ *A red admiral butterfly larva hangs from a leaf ready to pupate. Many butterflies and moths pass the winter as pupae, emerging in the spring. Some pupae have antifreeze chemicals in their blood. The relative length of day and night and the temperature determine whether the caterpillars produce a short-lived pupa (in early summer) or an overwintering one, and also determine when the butterfly emerges.*

14

The caterpillar then wriggles out of the old cuticle. It swallows air to make itself bigger and stretch the new cuticle before it hardens. The cuticle will still be a little wrinkled, to allow for more growth before the next molt.

The caterpillar will go on molting and growing as long as a special gland produces what scientists call a juvenile hormone. If the gland stops making this hormone, usually after about four normal molts, a different molt takes place. At this molt, the new cuticle become very hard, forming a protective case. Inside this case the great change from caterpillar to butterfly will take place. This special stage in the caterpillar's life is called the pupa. Before this molt the caterpillar becomes restless and may wander to find a suitable place to form into a pupa.

Many pupae are protected simply by their hard cuticle. This may be camouflaged to blend with the background or hidden in the soil, in a bark crevice or in rolled leaves sealed with silk. A few brightly colored pupae are poisonous and remain exposed.

▼ *The monarch butterfly is shedding its skin and turning into a pupa. You can see the developing wings of the adult butterfly, which were already growing under the old larval skin.*

The time between when the caterpillar stops feeding and the shell of the pupa hardens—usually about sixty hours—is a period of rapid change. During this time the caterpillar must find a suitable place to pupate. It also gets rid of all its waste and shrinks in size.

▶ *A monarch butterfly pupa hangs from its silk button. Soon the pupa will darken and become better camouflaged.*

▼ *As well as a silk pad, this black swallowtail pupa also has a silk girdle to hold it in place. Note the long, trailing antennae draped over the eyes of the butterfly forming inside it.*

The special gland stops making juvenile hormone, triggering all the changes that will transform the caterpillar into a free-flying butterfly. Clusters of cells in its body, which have been lying dormant since the caterpillar was first developing in its egg, start to multiply. These will form the wings, jointed legs, antennae, compound eyes, proboscis, and reproductive organs. At the same time the old organs that are no longer needed—the chewing mouth parts, stumpy prolegs, huge digestive system, and eventually the silk-spinning glands—start to break down. Special scavenging cells in the blood feed on the dying cells, and their waste products feed the growing cells of the butterfly. In this way, nutrients are transferred from the old organs to the new.

A new skin grows under the old caterpillar skin. Eventually the old skin is shed, and the new skin begins to harden. It is waxy to prevent water loss, because the pupa cannot absorb water. Now the first traces of the adult butterfly can already be seen: the faint triangular outlines of the wings and the pale spheres on either side of the head where the compound eyes are growing. Soon the pupa will darken, and this miracle of transformation will be hidden.

A silk moth cocoon cut open to show the pupa inside. The silk from silk moth cocoons is spun into cloth. Many moth caterpillars spin fluffy silk cocoons, sometimes adding pieces of bark for camouflage.

THE GREAT CHANGE

Inside the pupa, the drastic changes continue, and much of the insect's body appears to be a kind of thick soup, as old structures break down. The muscle system changes to service a flying, sucking insect instead of a crawling, chewing one. The true legs of the caterpillar develop into the slender, jointed ones of the adult. The wings, which had already increased in size eightfold by the time the pupa hardened, grow more and more. But how does the developing butterfly produce the intricate patterns and shimmering colors?

How the Butterfly's Wings Grow

These diagrams show a cross-section through a pupa. The wings develop from the inner layer of the old caterpillar skin, a part which is not shed. Groups of wing cells grow inward to form a small pocket.

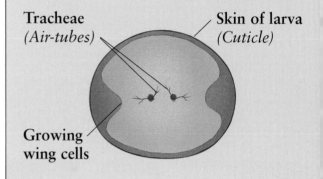

Tracheae
(Air-tubes)

Skin of larva
(Cuticle)

Growing wing cells

◀ *The red admiral butterfly inside this pupa is almost ready to emerge. Hidden from view underneath a nettle leaf, it has survived unharmed.*

The coloring of the butterfly's wings inside the pupa is a remarkable process. The scales are really special hairs produced by certain cells in the wings. At first they look like tiny bubbles on the ridges of the wings. Then they become larger and flatter and start to develop the microscopic ridges and curves that produce some of the colors.

They then start to grow outward again to form little bulges, the wing "buds." An air-tube or trachea from the thorax starts to grow into each bud. This will form the veins of the new wing.

Tracheae start to branch

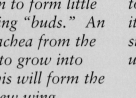

Cells move to area of growing wing

The wing eventually starts to flatten, and grow out of its pocket to lie on the surface of the body, just under the cuticle.

Tracheae forming "veins" of developing wing

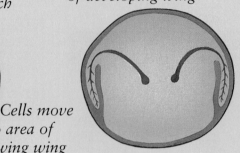

At about this time the new cuticle of the pupa forms, to protect the forming butterfly when the old caterpillar cuticle is shed. The changes described have taken just twenty-four hours to complete.

Hard cuticle forms to protect pupa

Wing

The next step in this process is the adding of other colors as chemicals—pigments. Waves of colored pigments are released into the blood. Only scales at the right stage of development can receive the pigments. By controlling the timing of pigment release and the rate of development of each scale, the butterfly controls the pattern of colors on its wings. The whole coloring process takes only about three days.

▶ *A close-up view of the wing scales of the elina moth from South America. The colors in a butterfly's wings are formed while it is in the pupa.*

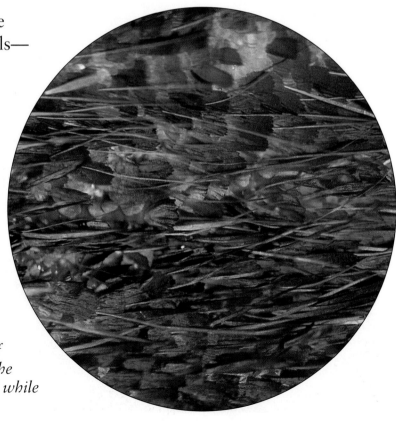

TAKING FLIGHT

The time it takes for a caterpillar to develop into a butterfly inside the pupa varies enormously. Some species take just a few days, while others may take a year or more. These are usually butterflies or moths that pass the winter in a resting stage as a pupa.

In the last few hours before the adult butterfly or moth emerges, you can often see the colors and patterns of the wing and body through the cuticle. When the butterfly is ready to emerge, the pupal skin usually splits at a special weak place on the thorax, and the butterfly escapes. Unlike butterflies, which emerge directly from the pupal skin, moths may have a cocoon, spun out of silk, from which they must escape.

Some moths secrete a special chemical to dissolve the silk. Others leave an opening in the cocoon, designed like a one-way valve, so that enemies cannot get in but the adult can get out. Still others, such as the luna moth, are strong enough to tear open the cocoon.

A red admiral butterfly breaks out of its pupal case and gets its first view of the world. Its large compound eyes give it almost all-round vision. Each eye is made up of thousands of tiny lenses.

◄ *Not all moths fly away. The female vaporer moth is wingless. She attracts a mate with her scent, then lays her eggs on her cocoon. The larvae will drift away on the wind on silken parachutes.*

Once the butterfly has emerged, it must find a suitable place to expand its wings. There it pumps blood into its wing veins to expand the wings until all their wrinkles are smoothed out. The cuticle then hardens, and the wings are stiff. The butterfly expels a droplet of reddish liquid, the waste that had built up inside while it was a pupa. It is now ready to fly away.

▶ *The newly-emerged red admiral butterfly rests on the empty pupal case while its wings expand and harden. Its furry body helps it to warm up and gain enough energy to fly away.*

THE WORLD OF THE BUTTERFLY

The adult butterfly or moth has a single purpose in life: to produce the next generation. Its powers of flight enable it to seek out mates, find food plants and new places to colonize, and seek shelter from bad weather. To sustain its energy-consuming flight, the butterfly feeds mostly on nectar, an energy-rich sugary liquid produced by flowering plants.

High-speed flight requires good eyesight. The fields of view of the compound eyes overlap, giving the insect stereoscopic (3-D) vision for judging speed and distance. These eyes are particularly good at detecting movements—an important aid for avoiding predators. The butterfly can detect wavelengths of ultraviolet light that we cannot see. Many flowers have ultraviolet guidelines to direct the butterfly to the nectar. Color vision also helps the butterfly recognize flowers and potential mates by their colors and patterns.

A butterfly also has a good sense of taste through special cells all over its body, especially on its feet and on the palps on each side of the proboscis. These help

A high brown fritillary feeding on nectar. When the butterfly's feet detect nectar, the long, tube-like proboscis unrolls automatically. Most butterflies and moths do not drink water—they get all the moisture they need from their liquid food. Some butterflies feed very little as adults, and silk moths do not feed at all, living entirely off their body fat.

▲ *A monarch butterfly in flight. The forewings provide the power for flight, while the hindwings are used for gliding, steering, and braking. The mechanism of flight is not like that of birds. The upper edge of each wing is attached to the inside of the thorax at a point that acts like a pivot point (fulcrum). When muscles pull this edge down, the wing rises. The underside of the wing is attached to a flexible membrane on the outside of the thorax. Muscles farther inside the thorax pull on this surface to drag the wing down. The shape of the wings causes them to flex during flight, giving lift and forward propulsion.*

it to find food and also to make sure that it lays its eggs on the right plants. It also has thousands of smell sensors on each antenna. Special hairs on the cuticle give it the sense of touch. Touch sensors near the base of each antenna monitor how much the antennae are

moved by the air as the butterfly flies, giving a measure of its speed. Other touch sensors on the joint surfaces tell it the position of its body parts.

▶ *Butterflies puddling on a muddy riverbank in Argentina. These butterflies seek minerals in puddles, mud, or a spot where an animal has urinated. Such gatherings are often entirely of males; the minerals may be needed to produce sperm, or the gatherings may serve to attract females.*

FINDING MATES

The brilliant color and patterns of butterfly wings seem designed for display. Even somewhat drab butterflies may have striking ultraviolet patterns that humans cannot see. Butterflies use color to recognize members of their own species and of the opposite sex, especially from a distance, but scent plays an even more important role in attracting a mate.

Special scent chemicals called pheromones give very specific signals to other insects. Many female butterflies and moths release pheromones that attract males from considerable distances. The smell sensors are on the antennae. They trap air in tiny chambers to analyze it. The female smoky moth's scent is so powerful that males may cluster around her cocoon before she has even emerged, and she may be mated before her wings have expanded.

The male emperor moth has the most acute sense of smell of any animal. Its smell sensors, 17,000 on each antenna, can detect a single molecule of female pheromone. This is enough to smell a female 6.8 miles (11 km) away, even though she releases just one-billionth of a gram an hour.

◀ *Once the female is persuaded to alight nearby, males of some species, such as this tiger moth, exude pheromones from tufts of bristles, called hair pencils, at the tip of the abdomen, which help persuade her to mate.*

The males of some species defend a territory around prominent landmarks in the vicinity of suitable food plants for the larvae, chasing away other males. Large groups of males of other species display together, or hold territories within a communal display ground.

Male butterflies also use scent in courtship. Some have special scales that release aphrodisiac chemicals. When courting, they release a shower of these scales, called "love dust," over the female. Other pheromones act to ward off competitors.

▶ *Behavior and touch are also used during courtship. Special postures bring the female's antennae into contact with areas of scent on the male's wings. This female heliconia butterfly (lower) is raising her abdomen to signal to the male (upper) that she has already mated. This saves them both time and energy.*

SURVIVING TO LAY EGGS

Once mated, the female butterfly flies off to lay her eggs. She selects a suitable food plant first by its particular shade of green, and then, on closer inspection, by its smell and taste. She avoids plants on which she can smell the presence of other caterpillars or eggs. Of course, the adult butterfly or moth must survive long enough to lay her eggs. She faces a host of enemies, from birds by day and bats by night to frogs, toads, lizards, spiders, and even other insects like the praying mantis.

Butterflies and moths use an astonishing range of defenses to outwit the enemy. Many moths and butterflies rely on bluff or deceit. As with caterpillars, camouflage is common, with adults often resembling tree bark, dead leaves, and even living green leaves with holes in them. Postures reinforce these effects. The pine beauty moth rests head down in young pine buds, resembling a tiny brown cone.

Some moths and butterflies, such as the clearwing moths, mimic wasps and bees, with yellow-and-black striped bodies and pinched, slender, wasp-like waists.

◄ *This Central American moth looks very much like a wasp, with its striped body and transparent wings. Very few predators will risk attacking it.*

◀ *This African butterfly looks as if it has a large head with long, thick antennae and shorter, curved legs, but these features are really streamers from the tips of its wings. They also have large, dark eye spots to complete the effect. Predators will attack the wings instead of the vulnerable head.*

Other butterflies have false heads—that is, the tips of their wings have antenna-like streamers with a dark, head-like pattern at the base to deflect attacks away from the vulnerable head area.

By surprising the enemy, an insect can often gain enough time to make its escape. Many butterflies and moths have large eye spots on their hind wings. When disturbed, they flash open their wings, revealing what appear to be the eyes of a much larger animal.

▶ *The huge owl butterfly, with a wingspan of over 5 inches (12.5 centimeters) display two huge owl-like eye spots on its wings as it rests.*

AMAZING BUTTERFLIES

Butterflies and moths are capable of some remarkable feats. Some fly thousands of miles from one continent to another and back. The painted lady butterfly migrates from North Africa to northern Europe, but only a few make the return journey. The monarch butterfly thrives in summer as far north as southern Canada, but it cannot survive the severe winter there. Millions of monarchs migrate south to coastal California and Mexico each autumn. The next spring, they make their way north again, breeding as they go, so a different generation returns.

Monarch butterflies at a winter roost in Mexico. One hundred million spend winter in Mexico, and five million spend winter in California. When migrating, they fly at heights of over 3,000 feet (1,000 m). They can cover 80 miles (130 km) a day for days on end. One female was recorded traveling a total of 2,133 miles (3,432 km). A few may even be blown on the wind to the shores of England, on the other side of the Atlantic Ocean, 3,400 miles (5,500 km) away.

How do they find their way? Butterflies use the position of the sun as a compass. They can also detect polarized light—changes in the light waves as they are filtered through clouds—so they can navigate even on a cloudy day. Moths can find their way in the dark. Many have a special reflective layer in the eye to increase light absorption. Like butterflies, they can use geographical landmarks, such as cliffs, even in the dark, and some can use spots of light, such as those formed by stars in the night sky. Some even use changes in the earth's magnetic field to guide them.

For humans, butterflies and moths can be both friends and foes. Armyworms, cotton bollworms, and other moth caterpillars destroy vast quantities of crops and defoliate forests. The larva of the clothes moth is an all-too-familiar pest, and the larvae of many butterflies, such as the cabbage white, turn prized green vegetables into useless lacy skeletons. But many butterflies and moths are valuable pollinators, and without them many plants would not set seed and many fruits would never be produced. Pollen brushes off on the butterfly's furry body as it feeds and is rubbed off on the next flower it visits. Without colorful butterflies there would be fewer colorful flowers.

A moth takes avoiding action as a bat approaches. Some moths have hearing organs specially tuned to the sound frequencies of their main enemy, bats. Bats hunt by sending out high-pitched squeaks and listening for the echoes from objects such as moths. The moths pick up these squeaks and plunge toward the ground as a bat approaches.

GLOSSARY

antennae: a pair of whip-like feelers on the head of an insect that it uses to touch and to smell.

camouflage: a kind of disguise, usually using color, patterns, or shapes that help an animal blend in with its background, making it hard for predators to see it.

colonize: to invade and live in a new area.

cocoon: a silky case which some larvae spin around themselves for protection during the pupal stage.

cuticle: the tough outer layer of an insect that protects the softer tissues inside.

gland: a cluster of cells that produces a chemical for a specific purpose. For example, silk glands produce silk, a liquid that hardens when exposed to air.

hormone: a chemical produced by living cells that acts as a messenger to carry signals around the body. These signals may tell an animal to start reproducing, to hibernate, or to migrate, for example.

larva (plural larvae): a young animal that hatches from an egg and looks very different from its parents.

palps: tiny, leg-like mouthparts used to touch and taste food.

pheromones: special scent hormones used by animals to communicate with each other. Different pheromones carry different messages.

pigment: a complex chemical that reflects light. Pigments in cells make those cells appear to be the color that they reflect. For example, leaves contain a pigment that reflects green light, so they appear green.

pollination: the placing of pollen from the male parts of one flower onto the female parts of another flower of the same kind. This must happen before the flower can produce seeds.

predator: an animal that hunts and eats other animals.

pupae: (plural pupae) the stage of an insect's life in which the larva (caterpillar) changes into the adult (butterfly). It is sometimes called a chrysalis.

sensor: a little cluster of cells that can detect certain things, such as touch, smell, or taste, and then send messages to the brain.

tissue: a large sheet, or cluster, of similar cells that work together to carry out a particular task, for example muscle tissue, or nerve tissue.

FURTHER READING

Crewe, Sabrina. *The Butterfly.* (Life Cycles). Austin: Raintree/Steck Vaughn, 1997.

Everts, Tammy, and Bobbie D. Kalman. *Butterflies and Moths (Crabapples).* Niagara-on-the-Lake, Ont., and New York: Crabtree Publishing Company, 1994.

Feltwell, John. *Butterflies and Moths (Eyewitness Explorers).* New York: Dorling Kindersley, 1997.

Gibbons, Gail. *Monarch Butterfly.* New York: Holiday House, Inc., 1991.

Grace, Eric S. *World of the Monarch Butterfly.* San Francisco: Sierra Club Books, 1997.

Opler, Paul. *Familiar Butterflies of North America (Audubon Society Pocket Guide).* New York: Knopf, 1990.

Sovak, Jan. *Learning About Butterflies (Learning About Books).* New York: Dover Books, 1997.

INDEX

Numbers in *italic* indicate pictures

$22.79

DATE			

MAR   2000